The **Essential** Buyer's Guide

Triumph
TR6

Your marque expert: Roger Williams

VELOCE PUBLISHING
THE PUBLISHER OF FINE AUTOMOTIVE BOOKS

www.veloce.co.uk

For post publication news, updates and amendments relating to this book please visit www.veloce.co.uk/books/V4026

First published in May 2006 by Veloce Publishing Limited, Veloce House, Parkway Farm Business Park, Middle Farm Way, Poundbury, Dorchester, Dorset, DT1 3AR, England. Reprinted January 2014.
Fax 01305 250479/e-mail info@veloce.co.uk/web www.veloce.co.uk or www.velocebooks.com.

ISBN: 978-1-845840-26-6 UPC: 6-36847-04026-0

Introduction
–the purpose of this book

The purpose of this book is to offer a reasonably quick step-by-step guide to finding a Triumph TR6 matched to your budget and ambitions. The task is not as easy as it sounds if only because owners' descriptions are often over-optimistic and some cars have lots of problems hidden under their seductive exterior. We therefore need to sort the wheat from the chaff.

Whatever the standard of car you seek, it will be out there. Finding it and helping you pay a fair price for it is the primary objective of the book. However, you need to start by making two decisions, the first of which is what you are prepared to pay.

Take care – you'll need to cross check

TR6s always look good and Dan Masters' is a superb example of the CC model. The Minilite wheels look great but are non-standard/stock, as are the extra driving lights.

prices carefully against the value tables in many of the various classic car magazines available and by looking at several cars, to ensure you have not set yourself an impossible task for a given budget.

Nothing beats viewing cars, asking questions and getting the feel of the market. Many vendors may rate you as a time waster if you give their car a 15 minute once over without buying, but it is essential you view a number of cars that seem to fall into your price and condition target before actually getting your wedge out of the bank! If you like what you see you can always take a few pictures and return to carry out a serious evaluation at a later date.

Along with the price issue is the question of whether to buy privately or from a dealer. So – what is your safety net position? Put another way, how much redress do you want? This can only be assessed by each individual and many will be happy to pay more to a reputable dealer, comfortable in the knowledge that if anything goes wrong they can pick up the phone and easily get help. Buying from a private vendor may save you some money, but there is little legal redress.

Particularly if going the private route, be prepared to travel long distances and still be disappointed. There will be several frustrating trips where you feel the vendor was wasting your time, but the right car *is* out there and will make it all worthwhile when you find it, so be patient and persistent.

The TR6 enjoyed a 7 year life from 1969 to 1976 – the longest production run of all the TRs. The car is the result of the Karmann company's clever redesign of the existing TR250/TR5 body. Although the external boot/trunk and bonnet/hood shapes were changed significantly, beneath the apparent major changes the TR6 bodyshell was actually very similar to the preceding models.

The TR6 was produced in two versions: the de-tuned US model and the sportier UK/RoW offering. The situation is complicated by the fact that both versions were further de-tuned in late 1972, and (on US models) the first anti-pollution equipment was introduced. However, the post-1972 models enjoy the much improved (but still not entirely foolproof) chassis and the sturdier and more reliable 'J' type gearbox. Furthermore, overdrives were fitted far more frequently to post-1972 cars.

Thanks

I am indebted to Dan Masters who helped with numerous US details, and to Derek Graham of the TR Register who helped me get my facts right.

Essential Buyer's Guide™ currency

At the time of publication a BG unit of currency "●" equals approximately £1.00/US$1.62/Euro 1.20. Please adjust to suit current exchange rates.

The TR6's 6 cylinder engine is torquey and sounds good. This particular engine is fuelled by the Lucas petrol injection system fitted as standard to the CP model.

Contents

1 Is it the right car for you?
– marriage guidance

Tall and short drivers

Standard seat adjustment is reasonable and will suit all but exceptionally tall/short drivers.

Maximum seat back to clutch pedal distance is 1.01m/3ft. Maximum headroom above the seat cushion is 0.86m/2ft 10in.

Weight of controls

By today's standards, slow speed steering and the brake and clutch pedals will seem on the heavy side. The gear lever can be 'notchy', particularly in worn examples, but is perfectly driveable.

Will it fit the garage?

Length   3.937m/12ft 11in
Width   1.470m/4ft 10in

Interior space

Internal width of 1.232m/4ft 0.5in between doors is adequate. When folded the hood takes up much of the rear shelf.

Luggage capacity

A $0.16m^3/5.6ft^3$ boot/trunk necessitates the use of soft bags and there is extra capacity on the back cockpit shelf, accessed by fold-forward seats.

Running costs

The owner's/workshop manual provides a comprehensive list of maintenance jobs at 6000 and 12,000 miles (10,000 and 20,000km), most of which are DIY. However, if the car is little used it is best to change the engine oil and filter every 12 months.

Useability

Today, this is a fun, second car rather than a daily driver.

Parts availability

Numerous specialist suppliers on both sides of the Atlantic provide an excellent replacement parts service.

Parts costs

See chapter 2 for a more detailed list of new parts costs.

Insurance

Costs can be quite modest if arranged through a recognised club scheme by an older driver with an exemplary record, but many factors affect the final cost.

Investment potential

Prices have been softening over the last two years. A cheap car and a home restoration could enable you to cover all your buying and restoration costs in final value (rarely practical with most classic cars).

Foibles

The original petrol injection fuel pump is vulnerable to overheating (solution – replace with a modern Bosch efi pump). Worn or unlubricated rear suspension is prone to 'twitch' when changing gear. Clutch life, gear changing and reliability can be problematic if incorrect components are fitted, modifications have not been carried out and/or the hydraulic actuation components are not kept in first class order. The clutch can appear at fault when the crankshaft thrust washer is worn, allowing the crankshaft to move forward when the clutch is depressed. There is also a tendency for the tail to squat under hard acceleration.

With the standard/stock trim the car is well instrumented and aesthetically pleasing. The burr-walnut fascia seen in this shot is an additional aftermarket touch of luxury.

Plus points

Timeless good looks, real character and a beefy, throaty engine.

Minus points

Old fashioned design with separate body and chassis construction. The youngest TR6 is 29 years old at the time of writing, so there are inevitably going to be unexpected problems, irritations and repair bills.

Alternatives

Austin-Healey 3000, Jensen-Healey, MGC, Morgan Plus 8, Reliant Scimitar.

2 Cost considerations
– affordable, or a money pit?

Prices exclude taxes:

New mechanical parts

Clutch set	●x100
Front brake discs (each)	●x25
Front brake pads (Kevlar)	●x40
Exhaust excluding manifold	●x150
Stainless manifold & exhaust	●x380
Radiator (exchange)	●x120
Set reinforced hoses	●x20
Alternator (exchange)	●x41
Distributor (exchange)	●x112
Front shock absorbers (each)	●x25
Brake servo	●x120
Brake master cylinder	●x90
Rear brake shoes (set)	●x15
Rear slave cylinder (each)	●x30
Clutch master cylinder	●x40
Clutch slave cylinder	●x30
Cylinder head gasket	●x20
Unleaded cylinder head (exchange)	●x335
Gearbox/transmission rebuild	●x300
Overdrive rebuild	●x275
Differential rebuild	●x300

Rear hubs (exchange)	●x76
Starter motor (exchange)	●x75
Bosch PI fuel pump kit	●x193
Rebuild PI unit (exchange)	●x160
PI injectors (each, exchange)	●x25
Carburettor fuel pump	●x15
Replacement wheels (each)	●x100

Body parts

Front/rear wings/fenders (each)	●x180
Bonnet/hood	●x300
Door	●x260
Door skin	●x60
Boot/trunk Lid	●x200
Windscreen/windshield	●x60
Interior trim panel set – vinyl	●x150
Wool carpet set	●x170
Seat re-cover kit – vinyl	●x170
New leather-covered seats	●x700
New hood cover – vinyl	●x160
New hood cover – mohair	●x300
Pair new rear light clusters	●x350

The earlier 'A' type gearbox with, in this case, an overdrive unit fitted.

Buy a replacement clutch set from a reputable TR specialist/dealer.

Rear driveshafts each have two universal joints, which will wear and eventually need replacing with this version. Note the improved and highly recommended telescopic rear dampers.

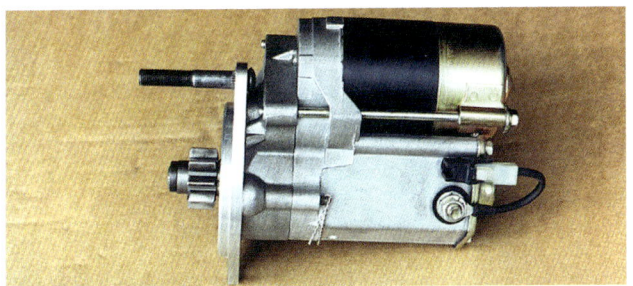

More expensive, certainly, but these modern starter motors are far more effective than an original replacement.

The differential, restrained from the top by two front and two rear pins.

3 Living with a TR6
– will you get along together?

If you love driving, you'll love the TR6, although it's really only a two-seater. I've known families travel quite long distances with the hood up and two children sitting on cushions on the back shelf, but, truth be told, buy a TR6 as a two-seater and you will not be disappointed. It's not a daily driver, but a high day and holiday car that is great fun to drive (preferably with the hood down), and which responds to being driven.

The suspension is hard compared to many cars of the same era, but even so the rear end will 'squat' under heavy acceleration, and this is usually countered by fitting even harder rear springs. The suspension with its (advanced for the time) independent rear arrangement affords the driver good control. Even so, firmer polyurethane bushes, particularly in the rear trailing arms, and better rear dampers improve the precision with which the car can be driven, resulting in extraordinary handling and grip from a 1960s car.

The car has a reputation for being the last of the hairy-chested sports cars, and I guess if you jumped out of your power-assisted, everything modern car into a TR6 for the first time, you might well endorse this view. On the other hand, my wife uses her TR6 every day, loves it and has never once complained that the clutch, brakes or steering are heavy. In fact, I think the '6 drives beautifully and the steering is a perfect blend of sensitivity and precision once you exceed walking pace. The brakes do pull the car up, but at today's motorway speeds they feel inferior to the modern cars that surround you so, in our case, I've upgraded the front calipers.

The clutch on the TR6 also has a reputation for fragility, and, sadly, I cannot argue the point. Later TR6s were fitted with a smaller clutch master cylinder to lighten the feel of the clutch pedal, but this also made the operation of the clutch mechanism marginal. In our case I fitted an earlier master cylinder which resolved the problem.

The petrol injection system on CP cars can be difficult to keep in optimum tune. It can lose its edge as the engine wears but is also frustrating to set up unless an aftermarket throttle linkage is fitted.

Furthermore, the original Lucas fuel pump should be replaced with an aftermarket version.

The car has other longevity shortcomings. All are well understood and proven modifications are available via the TR trade. One will catch out owners who 'ride the clutch' in traffic. The engine's crankshaft has inadequate thrust washers which wear under normal circumstances, but drivers who sit with their foot on the clutch will accelerate the problem and the need to rebuild the engine. That said, the engines are great – throaty-sounding with lots of torque, particularly from the early petrol injected CP model. The engines in the later CR and CF models are more docile but the '6's six cylinders are the ideal partner for the car.

Wire wheels, particularly chrome ones, really suit the TR6 but are very time-consuming to clean, and must be 72-spoke, heavy duty wheels to handle the stresses.

The gearbox has four forward speeds, the pre-1972 cars with synchromesh on three forward gears. Later cars have the better design of a 'J' four synchromesh unit, but you may be hard pushed to distinguish any other differences from the driver's seat. It surprises most enthusiasts to learn how few TR6s were fitted with overdrive. Today, overdrive is a necessity, not the highly desirable optional extra it once was. A good car with overdrive will sell very quickly and at a premium compared to a similar non-overdrive car.

Gear changing is clean and straightforward, if a little agricultural or notchy by today's standards. However, if you drain the oil when it's warm and replace the usual EP gear oil with a good quality 20/50 engine oil, you will transform the feel of the box. The one disadvantage is that you need to wait a few moments longer (to allow the spinning gears to slow down) before engaging reverse gear.

I did not find the original TR6 seats wonderfully comfortable, and long distances were, literally, a pain in the back. I changed the seats and the car is now a pleasure to drive all day. For those with long distance or long-term reliability doubts, we have covered long distances across the UK and Europe on numerous occasions (once or twice in appalling conditions) with no problems whatsoever.

However, the car is probably not best suited to owners unwilling to get their hands dirty from time to time. That said, I know several owners who know little about cars generally and get along with their TR6s in perfect harmony – with the aid of interested local garages. In general, though, when buying a 30-year-old car it's best if you enjoy fiddling/fixing/ maintaining cars, and the dirty hands (and satisfaction) that go with the work!

The ever-popular Minilite wheel offers owners the chance to personalise their cars, as does this frontal air dam fitted below the front bumper. The Minilites are lighter than the original wheels and thus improve road-holding, while the air dam improves cooling.

4 Relative values
– which model for you?

There is more detail on values in chapter 12 but this chapter expresses, in percentages, the relative value of the individual models in the USA and UK.

A number of repatriated warm climate cars come onto the UK market each year. Many remain in their original LHD condition, which devalues them. However, a number of these LHD cars have been converted to RHD. Even when the conversion has been carried out well, such cars do not attract the same value in the UK as an equivalent original RHD car. Where the conversion to RHD has been inexpertly carried out the value will be less than that stated below.

CP 150bhp petrol injection 1968-1972, 'A' Type 4 synchro gearbox with overdrive – **100%** (UK)
Non-overdrive – **90%** (UK)
CC carburettor 1969-1972, 'A' Type 4 synchro gearbox with overdrive LHD – **100%** (USA)
RHD – **90%** (UK)
Non-overdrive LHD – **95%** (USA)
Non-overdrive RHD – **80%** (UK)
CR 125bhp petrol injection 1973-1975, 'J' Type 4 synchro gearbox with overdrive – **90%** (UK)
Non-overdrive – **80%** (UK)
CF carburettor 1973-1976, 'J' Type 4 synchro gearbox with overdrive LHD – **100%** (USA)
RHD – **75%** (UK)
Non-overdrive LHD – **95%** (USA)
Non-overdrive RHD – **70%**(UK)

The following pictures should help you distinguish one model from the next.

The CP/CC dashboard had black instrument bezels and a rectangular wash/wipe switch mounted in the bottom right corner. Early cars had a central dashboard ignition switch without steering-lock, and hanging needles in the four smaller instruments. You can see the later upright needles on p41.

All pre-1973 models enjoyed clean, plain chrome bumpers front ...

CR models destined for the USA had these rather unsightly rubber over-riders fitted front and rear to comply with US collision regulations. This 1976 car must have been amongst the last produced by Triumph. Note the wipers park on the left of the screen and the all-amber front direction lights. The headlamps contain the side/parking-lights.

... and rear.

1973-on cars had a silver edge to the instrument bezels and the dials used a slightly different styling. The wash/wipe switch became square but remained mounted on the dash/fascia. The ignition key/lock varied by model and market. Initially on the centre-dashboard, all export cars from CC/CP50001 had a steering lock/column-mounted switch. For the UK a steering-locking switch was introduced from CP52786, but ¾ of CP/CC models had the lower steering column-mounted/locking item.

This UK CR model is finished in Sapphire Blue and has divided direction/parking lights – which, if you are looking for originality, are important. All TR6s were fitted with a chrome strip running along the sill/rockers between the wheels. The CR and their CF USA counterparts were fitted with a thicker chrome strip running along the sills/rockers between the wheels than the earlier CC/CP models.

This car is actually the preceding model to a TR6, but the interiors are identical. The central radio console has yet to be fitted, but this helps us assess the leg room which is more than adequate, although I found the TR6 seats unsupportive of my fragile back.

This view of the PI system enables us to ascertain that it has two sets of balance pipes and is thus a CR system as fitted to post-1973 European cars.

Under the bonnet/hood the petrol injection systems fitted to the CP and CR models varied in detail, but look very much alike from this side. The rocker cover is non-standard but nevertheless a useful replacement.

5 Before you view

– be well informed

To avoid the frustration of a car not matching your expectations, remember to ask specific questions when you call before viewing. Excitement about buying a TR6 can make even the most obvious things slip your mind, and it's harder for sellers to answer very specific questions dishonestly. Try to assess the attitude and demeanour of the seller, and decide how comfortable you are buying a used car from him or her.

Where is the car?

Work out the cost of travelling to view a car. For a rare model, or the exact specification you want, it may be worth travelling, but if your target is a common vehicle you should decide first how far you're prepared to go. Locally advertised cars can add to your knowledge for very little effort, so don't dismiss them.

Dealer or private sale

Is the seller the owner or a trader? Private owners should have all the history and be happy to answer detailed questions. Dealers may know less about a car, but should have some documentation and may offer finance. If a dealer offers no warranty or guarantee in writing, then why not buy privately and save money?

Cost of collection and delivery

Dealers may deliver but it probably won't be cheap. Private owners may meet you halfway, especially if the car is roadworthy, but be sure to view the car at the vendor's address beforehand to validate ownership and vehicle documentation.

Viewing – when and where?

It's always preferable to view at the vendor's home or business. A private seller's name and address should be on the title documents unless there's a good reason why not. Have at least one viewing in daylight and preferably dry weather. Most cars look better in poor light or when wet.

Reason for sale

Genuine sellers will explain why they are selling and their length of ownership. They may also know something about previous owners.

Conversions and specials

Many TR6s have returned to Europe from the USA. Conversion to RHD normally reduces their absolute value but makes them more saleable in the UK. Conversion can be easily verified as ID number suffixes differed between RHD and LHD. Check if headlamps, wiper pattern and sidelamp colour are correct for your market, as some safety inspections insist on this. Ask about the carburettors and compression, because

US market cars were given twin Strombergs, and the later CF cars anti-emissions equipment, mated to low-compression engines. They also had differently wired side lights.

Condition (body/chassis/interior/mechanics)
Query the car's condition in as specific terms as possible – preferably citing the checklist items described in Chapter 9.

All original specification
An unmolested original car is invariably of higher value and easier to get spares for than a customised vehicle.

Matching data/legal ownership
All TR6s have a chassis number, body number, engine number and gearbox number. All the numbers on the major parts and data plate should match to justify a top price, although changed engines, etc. noted on registration documents are acceptable, especially if the originals come with the car.

Does the vendor own the car outright or is money owed to a finance company or bank? Might the car even be stolen? Do any necessary finance checks before buying. Such companies can often also confirm if the car has ever been an insurance write-off. In the UK, the following organisations can supply vehicle data:

HPI   01722 422 422
AA   0870 600 0836
DVLA   0870 240 0010
RAC   0870 533 3660

Other countries will have similar organisations.

Roadworthiness
Does the car have all necessary certificates and/or comply with emissions rules? Test status for UK cars can be checked by phoning 0845 600 5977. Similar checks are available in some other markets.

If required, does the car carry a current road fund licence/license plate tag?

Unleaded fuel
As they left the factory all TR6s had what we now know as soft valve seats, unsuited to modern unleaded fuels. However, hardened inserts are now available and it has become common practice to have cylinder heads of this era converted for use with unleaded fuels, so you should ask whether the car you are viewing has been converted. If so, ask to see the receipt.

If you are looking at a petrol injected TR6, there will a second major component with which modern unleaded fuels are not entirely compatible: the seals used in the original metering units. If the metering unit has been professionally overhauled in the last few years there is a high probability that the seals will be unleaded compatible.

Ideally, the receipt will state that an unleaded conversion and recalibration overhaul have been carried out.

Do not overlook that TR6 fuel lines were made from sections of steel pipe joined by short lengths of flexible rubber hose. These lengths of hose also need to be upgraded to unleaded compatible rubber.

Insurance
If intending to drive the car home, check with your existing insurer in case your current policy does not cover you. It's wise to check insurance costs before purchase in any case, as TR6s are valuable and fast cars.

How you can pay
A cheque/check will take several days to clear and the seller may prefer to sell to a cash buyer. Cash can also be a valuable bargaining tool. However, a banker's draft or money order may be as good as cash, so ask beforehand.

Buying at auction?
See Chapter 10.

Professional vehicle check
TR6s are not complex cars by today's standards. Nevertheless, there are some important checks that should be made. If you feel unsure about making these checks yourself there are often marque/model specialists who will undertake professional examination of a vehicle on your behalf. Owner's clubs will be able to put you in touch with such specialists.

Other organisations that will carry out a general professional check in the UK are:

AA   0800 085 3007 (motoring organisation with vehicle inspectors)
ABS   0800 358 5855 (specialist vehicle inspection company)
RAC   0870 533 3660 (motoring organisation with vehicle inspectors)

Other countries will have similar organisations.

6 Inspection equipment
– these items will really help

This book
This book is designed to be your guide at every step, so take it along and use the check boxes in Chapter 9 to help assess each area. Don't be afraid to let the seller see you using it.

Glasses (if needed)
Take your reading glasses if you need them to read documents and make close up inspections.

Magnet (not powerful, a fridge magnet is ideal)
A magnet will help you check if the car is full of filler, or has fibreglass panels, but be careful not to damage the paintwork. It is a rule of TR6s that the rust you see is always far less than the hidden rust you cannot see. There's nothing wrong with a fibreglass bonnet/hood or boot/trunk lid apart from the lowered value and sometimes paint finish. You will find the magnet particularly useful at the point where body panels meet. See Chapters 7 and 9 for a more comprehensive breakdown of the locations particularly vulnerable to corrosion, and where, consequently, body filler is popular.

Probe (a small screwdriver works very well)
A small screwdriver can be used – with care – as a probe, particularly on the inner and outer sills, rear lower quarters, boot/trunkfloor, and anywhere around the bulkhead/firewall and battery tray to check any areas of corrosion.

Overalls
Be prepared to get dirty; take some overalls for getting under the car.

Mirror on a stick
Fixing a mirror at an angle on the end of a stick can help check the condition of the underside of the car and some of the important areas around the chassis. You can also use it, together with a torch, at several points on the chassis and bodywork, detailed in Chapters 7 and 9. A full on-ramp inspection is ideal.

Digital camera
If possible, take a digital camera for reference or to study known trouble spots later. Show an expert pictures of any part that causes you concern. Ideally, have a friend or knowledgeable enthusiast accompany you: a second opinion is always valuable.

Go for a short run. Do not worry about the tune or acceleration or finer details – we are initially looking for expensive problems. The car must pull up straight on the brakes; not puff out smoke from the exhaust; change gear without bulking or grating; steer straight with hands off the steering wheel, and not emit any unpleasant noises from the engine or differential areas.

Try the gearbox briefly in each of the four gears, concentrating for now on testing each gear on over-run. The gear should stay engaged, if it pops out the gearbox is worn. If overdrive is fitted, try flicking the 'in' switch with the car in top gear at about 50mph/80kph – it should snap in. They always drop out quickly so that is no test, but a worn overdrive will usually take a few seconds to get up to pressure after the switch has been flicked 'in', which signals remedial action and cost in due course.

Exterior
An overall impression of the bodywork is best gained from the rear of the body. All TR's are longitudinally fish-shaped – there is a gradual side curve from front to back. So go to one rear corner and look down the coach line. The car should have a steady curve, just like a fish! Go to the other side of the car and check for the same. What you should be particularly wary of is one very curvaceous side and one flat side. This signals a knock, poor rebuild, or even a front half/rear half marriage from two different cars. The latter is not a complete no-no, but needs to have been carefully, and therefore invisibly, carried out.

Unless the car is very cheaply priced, most buyers should walk away if the two sides do not curve equally.

Before you move away from the rear of the car check whether you can see the rear chassis crossmember. Hopefully the rear valance will be covering it. If you can see it, the rear of the chassis will have been incorrectly repaired and will need further 'body-off', and thus expensive, correction.

Check each of the four wing/fender panel joints (i.e. where one panel interfaces with the next) for rust, paint bubbling or signs of local repair. More

Wings/fenders should have been painted OFF the car. Although most soft sealer will have squeezed out as the wings were bolted up, there should still be evidence of it. If you cannot see the sealer ...

... presume corrosion damage at least to this level.

importantly, check that the interface is visible and has not been overlaid and hidden with body filler. The rear wing/rear deck joints, one each side of the car outboard of the fuel filler, are particularly worth studying. In addition to an absence of rust you are looking for signs of a soft sealer having been coated on the panel faces before the wing/fenders were bolted to the shell.

Check (carefully) the bottom of the doors for corrosion.

While you are making these specific checks, take a few seconds to survey the overall quality of the paintwork.

Check whether there is a hood frame. The quality of the hood itself is immaterial at this stage.

Under-bonnet/hood

Lift the bonnet and check down the gutters each side of the bonnet/hood lip. You are looking for an absence of corrosion and signs of a soft sealer having been applied before the wing was bolted in place. Leave the bonnet up but move to the rear of the car and lift the boot/trunk lip. Use your torch to look first then very carefully run your hand over the outer edges of the inner wheelarches as far forward as you can, looking for corrosion. Take a look at the floor of the boot/trunk, which is very vulnerable to corrosion.

If the doors are in this condition, they are repairable but do you really want the bother?

At the front of the car look down just inboard of the inner wings at the front suspension pillars, their angled supports, and as much of these parts of the chassis as you can see. Corrosion, signs of patching, any distortion (accident damage), or

Colour and quality of the paintwork is crucial. Here, the quality is superb. This looks like Pimento Red – an original Triumph colour. In fact, Dick Taylor whispered to me that it is sprayed Porsche Guards Red, and thus would not be a good buy if you had concours d'elegance competitions in mind.

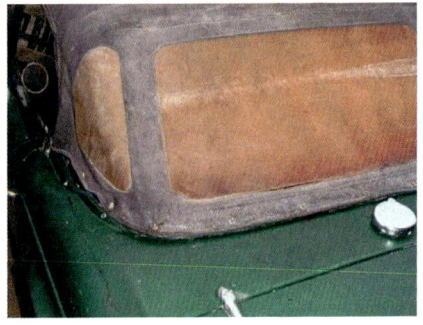

A new hood is clearly required – but if the rest of the car is to your requirements, do not let this put you off.

An excellent example of a TR6 engine bay. Clearly a 'hot' car from the look of (not to mention the expense of) the triple Weber DCOE carburettors. I would really enjoy this car, but is it for you? The rocker cover is a cast alloy aftermarket fitting intended to reduce tappet noise, and the oil leaks which are fairly common from the original pressed covers.

even holes here are bad news because rectifying involves removing the body from its chassis.

While you've got your head in the engine bay and have torch in hand, make a note of the engine number. If it begins 'CP' the car should be a petrol injected TR6 registered up to late 1972. Does that check out with what the owner says he is selling?

'CC' will indicate a US TR6 to late 1972, fitted with carburettors.

'CR' should mean you've come to see a 125bhp petrol injected car made between 1973-1976.

'CF' will have been fitted to a US TR6 made during or after 1973 and fitted with carburettors.

If the engine prefix does not match the supposed origin of the car, the originality value can be adversely affected, but perhaps not severely. However, the six-cylinder engine has a crankshaft thrust bearing weakness (more details and a test can be found on p23) that occasionally necessitates a replacement engine. On occasions similar engines are imported from Triumph's saloon cars. This should not affect the way the car performs but such a substitution does detract from the car's value so watch for all non-CP, -CR, -CC, or -CF prefixes, particularly MG, MN, MM and MP. These engines will have come from 2.5PI, 2.5PI, 2.5TC and 2500S saloon donors respectively.

All well so far? OK, time to get the overalls on and look under the car.

Underneath
Start by lying alongside the car just aft of the front wheels, and carefully run your hand along the flat of the chassis. You are feeling for two things – that the chassis is free of scale and corrosion generally, and any sign of ridging caused by an accident. If you notice anything untoward, take a close look.

Now for the most difficult place to access, but one of the TR6's most vulnerable corrosion traps. To get at it you need to either jack the rear of the car and securely place axle stands under it, or drive the rear onto a pair of inspection ramps. Take your torch and, if the current owner agrees, a small prodder (a screwdriver is ideal) and get yourself close to the 'T-shirt' (you will see why when you get there) pressing where four pieces of chassis meet just in front of the differential. Take your time for you must be sure all the chassis members are free of serious corrosion. The T-shirt pressing is a highly stressed part of the chassis, as are the arms that radiate away from it carrying the trailing arm rear suspension. Repairs here are the job of professional TR restoration businesses and consequently are expensive.

Look outboard of the T-shirt at the rear suspension mounting members. They are a major load-bearing part of the chassis so it is imperative they are in first class order along their full length.

Move backwards a step and look at the four mounting pillars that retain the differential to the chassis. Ideally, they should be boxed (a recognised strengthening technique for this weak spot) but many cars still have the original securing pillars, which is fine so long as they are not broken. Try to move the diff – it should be completely secure.

Come back another metre and take a close look at the chassis members and cross members over and to the rear of the differential. Look very closely and give all corroded areas a good prod to ensure solidarity. As you move towards the rear panel of the car, pay progressively more attention, as the chassis rots from the rear towards the centre T-shirt. Finally, take a look at the floor at the rear and take in as much of the rear wheelarches as you can during a quick evaluation. You are not covering all the corrosion spots at the rear of a TR6, but it is safe to say that if the ones you are able to check are in good condition, it is likely that the rest will be reasonable, too. However, be alert to the fact that if the parts you check are in poor shape, other less accessible areas are unlikely to be in any better order: significant remedial work and cost could be involved in rectifying the situation.

If you've got doubts, take an extra five minutes to remove a rear wheel. You can view the outer end of the top spring bridge and the rear chassis member, feel the driveshaft, view the damper and look around under the rear wing/fender. In this case the bonus would be to establish whether the damper link has broken off the end of the suspension arm, necessitating a replacement arm.

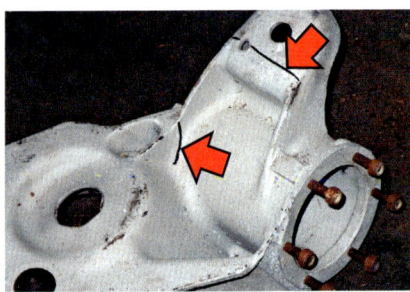

Trailing arms are prone to cracking in two places, marked here. You can see where the rear damper attachment point cracks then severs.

Interior

Still interested? Open the doors, take a quick look underneath them, lift the carpets in the footwells and check the four outer corners. Now drop forward one of the seats and lift the covering on the rear shelf. It should be unmolested. Signs of welding/patching almost certainly signal that someone has inexpertly repaired the differential mounting pins.

As you exit the interior, take a very quick look at the trim panels and carpets, although their condition should not influence your decision to meticulously explore the car.

Mechanics

The last of your quick checks is to ensure that the crankshaft end-float is not unreasonable. With the engine switched off and the bonnet/hood open, lever the front crankshaft pulley backwards as hard as you can. Get the vendor to jump in the car and press the clutch hard to the floor while you watch to ensure the front pulley does not move forward. If you see any movement, repeat the exercise but this time do so with a tape measure to hand to check the extent of the movement. Anything more that $\frac{1}{16}$in or 1.5mm means the float in the crankshaft requires attention, which can usually be resolved without removing the engine from the car. If the movement is excessive, start the engine and listen for a knocking/thumping when the clutch is depressed. If the movement is in the order of, say, $\frac{1}{4}$in or 6mm, you will hear a very unnerving thumping from the bottom of the engine. Budget for a replacement engine to be on the safe side – or walk away.

Paperwork

If you're still interested, this would be a good moment to check the registration document – the V5C in the UK and the pink slip in the USA. First off, ensure that the person you are talking to and the address you are visiting tally with the registration document ... and if they do not you will need a very convincing explanation to retain your interest. You need then to check that the chassis number and engine numbers not only correspond with the registration document, but are also compatible with the year of the car and its model number (CP, CC, CR or CF). You will find this information in Chapter 17.

Is it worth staying for a longer look?

Is the colour what you expected or can live with?

Does the paintwork seem acceptable to your requirements?

Does the bodywork seem sound – bearing in mind that a new body and subsequent paint restoration is very expensive?

Does the chassis seem sound – bearing in mind that chassis repair or replacement is a big job?

Are you really able to rectify any shortcomings you've noticed, or should you be taking advice about what is involved before you decide?

Although the easiest and least expensive to rectify, do the main mechanical components seem in reasonable order so far?

Are any shortcomings you have discovered reflected in the price?

Is your heart ruling your head? If so, come back after you've had time to think and maybe talk to a TR6 professional specialist. Best not to act in haste and repent at leisure!

Possibly the most important part of any TR6 is the structural integrity of the (normally hidden) chassis. The rear half seen here collects all the spray from both front and rear wheels, and consequently is the most vulnerable to corrosion.

These uneven door gaps warn you that this chassis is either structurally unsound or that the car has been appallingly restored.

These door gaps are more what you are looking for but do not guarantee a completely sound chassis.

Check out the book/trunk – the rear of the TR6 is vulnerable to rot so this standard of finish is reassuring.

Note the uniform panel gaps round the boot/trunk lid. This CF model has the number plate light in the boot lid, a clean rear bumper that is in superb condition, black rear panel, a superb PVC hood, and a crystal-clear rear window. Check out the rear lights – these are excellent. Replacements are available, but expensive.

The bumpers, wheels (non-standard/stock in this case) and tyres are important, but above all the colour and quality of the paintwork must meet your requirements.

You need to ensure the inside of the cockpit meets your standards. This is an exemplary CP dashboard.

The paint finish in the engine bay is important and will tell you much about the life the car has had, but the quality of the pipes and wiring and the manner of their installation is worth noting. This is an RHD petrol injected CP model, and a superb example.

9 Serious evaluation
– 60 minutes for years of enjoyment

It is hard to remember the detail of any car you inspect on a serious basis even an hour or two later, so circle the Excellent, Good, Average or Poor box of each section as you go along. The totting up procedure is detailed at the end of the chapter. Be realistic in your marking.

Paintwork

Ex   Gd   Av   Po

Assess the car's paintwork and decide whether it is right for you. Like bodywork shortcomings, paintwork can be very expensive to properly correct. It takes time to remove all chrome work, wings and fittings and carry out chemical stripping to bring the car back to bare metal – and this is all before the pre-paint preparation and actual painting can take place. You are looking at £2500 to £5000 to have the paintwork properly applied. Even new Heritage or rust-free Californian shells need to have the wings/fenders removed before painting in order to ensure the paint is applied to the mating surfaces and then re-assembled (with sealer) if you are to achieve a lasting impressive finish. Not to do the job correctly repeats the errors of Triumph back in the '60s and '70s and eventually renders useless much of the remedial bodywork repairs you may have already carried out.

You can help the situation by doing the stripping yourself. Remember as you go over the car that the cost of good paint will repay itself in due course, even though expensive in the short term.

Body panels
Overall structure

Ex   Gd   Av   Po

Go to one rear corner, kneel down and look along the coach line to ensure the body has a steady curve both sides, like a fish. One overly curvaceous side and one flattish side means a poor accident or restoration rebuild and the need for further major repair.

Body filler

Sadly, it is an inescapable fact that all TRs have a number of corrosion weak spots. Be alert to filler cover-ups anywhere in the car but particularly in the weak spots detailed in the following text. Each location should be examined carefully and a magnet used to test for body filler when in doubt. There used to be a tendency to mask corrosion by filling the gaps between all four wings and the sills. Regard with suspicion any car where there is no clear and obvious gap between each wing and its mating sill.

Rear deck panel and forward deck section

Ex   Gd   Av   Po

Bubbling below the paint will signal trouble in the near future. Note that top repairs can be effected quite professionally and hide, for a short while, the true seriousness of the situation, which is why an examination from inside the boot is particularly

Holed due to unseen corrosion at ends of rear deck and forward extensions.

This splash plate looks very good, but you can see how, once holed, spray can cause corrosion, often in the engine bay.

The same corrosion problem occurs at the rear.

valuable. Feel where the rear wing is bolted to deck sections alongside the fuel tank. On some cars there will be only daylight where the panel has completely rusted away.

Above and around the headlamps

Ex Gd Av Po

Corrosion works back to the inner wings where the bonnet hinges are mounted, so take a look from inside the engine bay.

Front valance

Ex Gd Av Po

Look at the front valance closely – it is attacked not only by corrosion but by kerbs and other raised objects. Body filler is often present, masking its true condition.

Splash plates

Ex Gd Av Po

Look at the plates behind the front wheels of course, but the serious corrosion manifests itself next to the fuse box on the inner wing. There is a similar weakness in front of the rear wheels.

Wing-to-body joints

Ex Gd Av Po

Regrettably, this was never originally painted and all four joints/interfaces corrode along their length. Any time you remove a wing/fender from the main bodyshell, apply both paint and sealer to all faces upon reassembly.

Bottom of doors

Run your hand carefully along the bottom where the door shell joins the outer skin. Rust can sometimes be obvious without the need to do this check.

Top of both doors

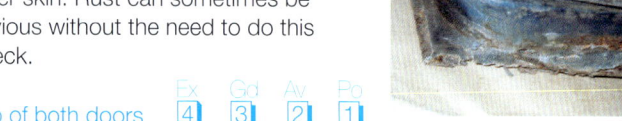

Ex Gd Av Po

The front of the doors where they sit adjacent to the windscreen panel is prone to corrosion and, aided by door glass movement, can also crack the top of either or both doors.

The headlamp recesses trap dirt, which retains water and keeps it in contact with the inner wing.

Triumph did not think paint was essential between wing/fenders and the main bodyshell.

The door skin turns over the bottom lip and rots, as does the bottom of the door shell.

The windscreen frame

This lightweight pressing is bolted to the scuttle, and can rust from the inside or crack due to loads imposed by the hood. The early stages of corrosion can only be seen when the screen is off the car, but take a close look anyway.

Rear wing attachment to 'B' post

This mating face usually rots from the bottom up.

Rear valance

Run your hand (carefully) along the whole bottom edge of the rear valance (particularly where the exhaust pipe exits) to check for corrosion. You would get a hint from the condition of the adjacent boot/trunk floor, which, if poor, would make you look closely at not only the rear valance but adjacent panels, too.

The boot/trunk lid

The lid is most vulnerable along the rear lip overhang where its double skin traps moisture and the exhaust gases vortex up, causing double corrosion problems. Repair is not viable and a new one is needed.

Boot/trunk floor

You may need to remove the spare wheel, but the floor is vulnerable to corrosion.

Rear inner wing

Check from inside the boot with the boot trim panels removed and by looking and feeling each side of the fuel tank.

Front wings/fenders

Corrosion or damage to a TR6 wing is best handled by fitting a new replacement wing (at about £180 each). They fit well and make the most economical repair.

This example is perfect but you will need to feel beside the fuel tank to find inner wing/fender corrosion.

The sills/rockers

These go in two places – the outside is usually pretty obvious and normally visible. However, the front wing/fender covers the first couple of feet and the sill/rocker can be disintegrating but hidden. Look closely at the inner sill/rocker, too, from inside the cockpit. The inner sill

The top front corners of the door corrode, too.

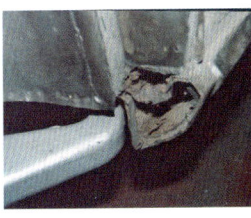

The front of the rear wing/fender attaches to the 'B' post and corrodes.

Note how the boot/trunk top lip slightly overhangs the rear panel, creates a vacuum, and sucks spray and exhaust fumes onto the back end of the boot lid.

forms part of the floor panel and outer sill corrosion of any severity is likely to manifest itself in at least the outer front corner.

The floors

Ex	Gd	Av	Po
4	3	2	1

Check the floors in the cockpit generally, but particularly at the four corners nearest each of the wheels.

Rear shelf

Ex	Gd	Av	Po
4	3	2	1

Tip both seats forward and check the rear shelf and its vertical face for both corrosion and, in the case of the shelf,

The front wing/fender hides corrosion occurring at the front of the sill/rocker.

This picture illustrates severe corrosion in the inner sill/rocker, floor and drain from the plenum.

The floors can corrode very severely.

any patches and unusual welding. The differential sits below the shelf and patching of the shelf is likely the result of a cheap, inexpert repair to the diff mounting pins.

This corroded rear shelf has been partially removed to reveal the crossmember.

Bonnet/hood

Ex	Gd	Av	Po
4	3	2	1

These corrode at the front where the double-skinned area is, and at both rear corners where owners have lifted the bonnet too enthusiastically and slightly raised the rear corner of the bonnet. You can even find a split about 12in (30cm) in front of the rear edge of the bonnet on some cars.

The plenum chamber

Ex	Gd	Av	Po
4	3	2	1

This double-skinned cavity goes across the full width of the car under the scuttle/windscreen, and can hold water entering the air vent of the scuttle. To detect problems look first for signs of water ingress on carpets and rust on the floor panels, and check with a good torch under the dashboard. This is a difficult repair which is expensive.

Battery trays

Ex Gd Av Po
[4] [3] [2] [1]

Battery acid corrodes these, but fortunately this is amongst the easier repairs. Look, too, under the brake/clutch master cylinders for corrosion from fluid stripping the paint.

Shut lines

Ex Gd Av Po
[4] [3] [2] [1]

Exclude the door gaps for a moment but check the evenness of the gaps between the bonnet/hood and wing/fender, the bonnet and scuttle, the boot/trunk lid and rear wing/fender, and the boot/trunk lid and rear deck. They should all be even and consistent.

The original side-engine oil filter gives rise to a short period of oil starvation on starting.

Seating comfort

Ex Gd Av Po
[4] [3] [2] [1]

How do the seats support your back? Do the seat backs (squabs) feel loose or nicely taut and supportive? Are the seat (base) cushions firm or do they feel as if the foam is reverting to powder and not giving you the support you expected?

Start-up
Cold start

Ex Gd Av Po
[4] [3] [2] [1]

Make a mental note of the car's cold starting characteristics as you start it for the first time.

Engine rattle

Ex Gd Av Po
[4] [3] [2] [1]

The position of the original oil filter gives rise to short term oil starvation upon start-up, characterised by an initial rattle. Does the car have a bad and worryingly prolonged rattle (rate 'poor'), or has a spin-on oil filter upgrade been fitted that eliminates the initial rattle, warranting excellent marks?

General condition

Ex Gd Av Po
[4] [3] [2] [1]

Blue smoke from the exhaust on starting signifies general wear and tiredness. Do the tappets rattle initially? Do the tappets rattle even with the engine is warm?

Crankshaft endfloat

Ex Gd Av Po
[4] [3] [2] [1]

Push the clutch to the floor and listen for any unusual (deep thumping) engine noises.

Chassis, suspension and underneath checks

Suggestion – unless you are exploring a very cheap restoration candidate, it is worth arranging a half hour session on the lift at a local garage/tyre centre. You can then check the following in safety and without having to scrabble around on the ground.

Door shut lines

Ex 4 Gd 3 Av 2 Po 1

TR6 door gaps open as the chassis structure weakens – thus wide and tapered gaps are bad news, and should alert you to question either the integrity of the chassis or if it has been poorly repaired. Check before moving off.

Rear chassis member

Ex 4 Gd 3 Av 2 Po 1

The end of the right-side chassis member tells us this has a 'hogged' chassis and requires body-off rectification.

Stand away from the rear of the car and check whether you can see the rear chassis crossmember protruding below the rear valance. If visible you can presume that the chassis has been incorrectly repaired. This is the infamous 'hogging', brought about by bad welding. A replacement chassis must be budgeted for – or walk away now.

Perfect door-shut gaps.

Rear suspension legs

Ex 4 Gd 3 Av 2 Po 1

The two chassis legs that connect the central cruciform/T-shirt to the outer chassis members, and carry the two trailing arms, are the first things to rot. They are a major load-bearing part of the chassis and it is imperative they are in first class order along their full length.

With the T-shirt pressing removed the full-length, very dangerous corrosion in this chassis leg is clear.

T-shirt pressings

Ex 4 Gd 3 Av 2 Po 1

The central chassis cruciform is located just in front of the differential into which the aforementioned chassis legs are welded. This junction is 'plated' top and bottom with diamond shaped pressings called in the trade 'T-shirt pressings'. When rusted metal is present underneath the pressings, they swell and delaminate, but most importantly lose their load-carrying capability. It is not unknown for a bodged repair to be done by plating over the top of the unsound rusted metal. A professional and properly executed repair is likely to set you back ●x750.

Front suspension mountings

Ex 4 Gd 3 Av 2 Po 1

Study the rear lower wishbone attachment brackets – they are a known weakness. It is acceptable that they have been welded (average points), but they MUST have been welded competently and have added strengthening gussets welded in place at the same time to qualify for good or excellent points.

At the top of the picture is a dangerously corroded chassis leg, while the holed T-shirt pressing shows that it offers no structural strength whatsoever.

Front suspension weaknesses are so common that strengthening kits are available.

Rubber bushes

Check the appearance of the rubber suspension bushes – awarding excellent marks only if they have been replaced with polyurethane bushes.

Steering

Check the obvious steering components (rack, ball-joints) for wear and the integrity of the various gaiters by rocking the steering back and forth. Also try and check that the steering rack mounting brackets welded to the chassis are not cracked; you may need a small, dentist-like mirror for this.

This would be an excellent rebuild had the owner fitted polyurethane suspension bushes instead of the rubber ones shown.

Frontal sidemembers

Find and check where the chassis goes from two side members to one, roughly underneath the 'A' or front door pillar. If the car has had significant accidental/frontal impact it will show here with a crease. If present closely examine the entire front of the chassis. Also check the integrity of the front turret braces.

Chassis repairs

Spliced or patched chassis repairs are not acceptable unless they have been very professionally carried out, in which case you could award average points. The best repair will be 'invisible' because that chassis member has been replaced in its entirety, attracting good or excellent points. While this applies right through the chassis pay particular attention to the rear where spray from all four wheels has subjected members to the greatest corrosion.

A very typically cracked steering-rack mounting bracket.

A superb front turret brace. Ensure yours are as sound as this one.

Chassis repairs are not ideal, but are to some degree inevitable, and must have been done professionally.

The differential mounting

Check the four mounting pillars that retain the differential to the chassis.

Push, pull and generally try to move the diff – it should be completely secure, in which case give the car an average mark. If the four pillars have been boxed give the car a good mark, or if beautifully carried out, an excellent mark.

A partially welded side/boxing plate on one of four differential mounting pins.

Rear spring bridge

Ex	Gd	Av	Po
4	3	2	1

This is away from convenient viewing but corrosion can result in the top spring cups breaking off, a rear spring being ejected through the top of the wing/fender, and loss of control of the car. Consequently, take your time to evaluate this important part as thoroughly as possible.

Boot/trunk support

Ex	Gd	Av	Po
4	3	2	1

Come back a step and take a close look at the chassis members and crossmembers over and to the rear of the differential. Look very closely and give all corroded areas a good prod to ensure their solidarity. As you move towards the rear panel of the car, pay progressively more attention, for the chassis rots from the rear forward.

Boot/trunk floor

Ex	Gd	Av	Po
4	3	2	1

Take this opportunity to study the floor panels, as much of the rear wheelarches as you can see, and the inside of the rear valance from the underside of the car.

Terminal corrosion in a rear spring bridge.

Rear suspension

Ex	Gd	Av	Po
4	3	2	1

The trailing arms are the main constituent of the rear suspension – check the four bushes and only award excellent marks if polyurethane replacements have been fitted.

This tubular crossmember supports the boot/trunk of the car and its spare wheel.

Rear shock absorbers

Ex	Gd	Av	Po
4	3	2	1

You can only visually check the rear dampers. Award excellent marks only if telescopic replacements have been recently fitted and 100 per cent of the stresses are carried by the chassis (NOT by bodywork).

The trailing arm mounting brackets are in view, along with the spring bridge and the top of two T-shirt pressings.

Driveshafts

Ex Gd Av Po
4 3 2 1

Check that the rubber gaiters are not split and that there is no obvious slop in the u/js (two per shaft), mindful that the outer u/js cannot be seen so you will have to twist each in turn. There should be slight signs of lubrication from the gaiters but no leaks. Only award excellent marks if new driveshafts with enlarged greasable u/js have been fitted recently.

Propeller shaft

Ex Gd Av Po
4 3 2 1

Check the propshaft u/js (two) for wear/play.

Oil leaks

Ex Gd Av Po
4 3 2 1

Check the differential seals (three) and the gearbox rear seal for oil leaks. Check the bottom of the bellhousing for excessive oil.

Clutch mechanism

Ex Gd Av Po
4 3 2 1

Check that the linkage is connected to the middle hole in the lever which is welded to the gearbox cross shaft. The clutch mechanism is vulnerable to wear: have the pedal depressed a few times whilst you watch each connection in turn for slop/wear. The fork or its pin can wear, and while one worn joint is unlikely to cause problems, several will cause difficulty in fully disengaging the clutch.

Exhaust system

Ex Gd Av Po
4 3 2 1

Visually check the exhaust system for corrosion, sound-looking joints and appropriate mountings. If in doubt, test it by having the engine run while you listen for 'blows'.

Rust proofing

Ex Gd Av Po
4 3 2 1

Last, but certainly not least, do check that the chassis member and the underside of the body show evidence of internal and external wax protection.

Test drive

Take at least thirty minutes over the return journey because it is an opportunity to assess the driving characteristics of the car.

Warm start

Ex Gd Av Po
4 3 2 1

Does it start well/quickly after standing?

Steering

Ex Gd Av Po
4 3 2 1

Does it steer straight (hands-off)?

You need telescopic rear dampers fitted via similar mounting brackets to these.

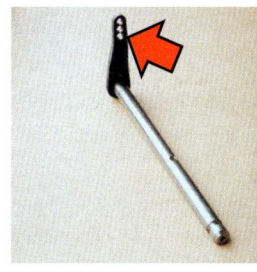

The TR6 clutch mechanism must be connected via the middle of these three holes.

Front shock absorbers

Assess their performance on a twisting and/or bumpy stretch of road.

The clutch/pedal

Does the pedal move and engage the clutch smoothly? Is the bite point about halfway up and consistent? Is there any clutch judder? If the clutch is stiff or heavy and partially ineffective, it is possible the clutch fork within the bellhousing has broken requiring gearbox removal to effect repair.

Foot brake operation

Check for effective operation. Brakes should inspire confidence and pull up the car up in a straight line. I would suggest you only award excellent marks to a car that has upgraded front calipers and disc/rotors.

Hand/parking brake

Does it hold the car securely on an incline? If so, try it on a hill. The handbrake on a TR6 is usually poor, and to gain excellent marks it will need to have been modified and be able to hold the car securely on a steep hill.

You'll not see these clutch components but poor/heavy clutch operation will alert you to the securing pin having broken.

Gearbox assessment (1)

Try the gearlever into each gear. It will require a firm action and also full clutch depression, but it shouldn't refuse to go into any gear, nor make complaining noises.

Gearbox assessment (2)

Try the gearbox in every gear on over-run (not in drive) for jumping out of gear. You can watch the gear lever for clues during the over-runs – a poor one will inch forward slightly before popping out.

Gearbox assessment (3)

Stop in a quiet spot and then listen while you drive slowly away in first gear. If the gearbox hisses it is likely that the layshaft needle roller bearings are picking up on the layshaft hardened surface, and will require replacement in due course. This is particularly bad news if the car is fitted with overdrive, for not only is it essential to overhaul the gearbox but the overdrive unit, too.

Gearbox release bearing

With the engine running and the gearbox in neutral while in your quiet spot, listen to see if the box hisses when the clutch is depressed. If so, the clutch release bearing must be suspect.

Overdrive fitted?

Only about 5 per cent of the CC versions of the TR6 and 70 per cent of the CP models were fitted with overdrive. The CF/CR versions did have overdrive far more frequently. Thus, overdrive is a very desirable feature, and deserves to be marked in the context that the outright sale of a reconditioned 'A' type box with overdrive will, in fact, set you back about ⬤x1000. A later 'J' type will be about half that cost – but remember you still have to have the gearbox fitted and that a new clutch is prudent – collectively an expensive rectification.

Overdrive operation

Ex | Gd | Av | Po
4 | 3 | 2 | 1

When the overdrive control switch is flicked on, the overdrive should cut straight in and with sufficient force to slightly jolt the car. An overdrive that is slow to come in is likely to be suffering a worn overdrive pump. Repairs cost ⬤x500, plus (nine times out of ten) the cost of a new clutch.

The differential

Ex | Gd | Av | Po
4 | 3 | 2 | 1

If the rear of the car 'thuds' when the clutch is let in or out it is invariably due to the right-hand front diff mounting pin having pulled out of its chassis mounting. The differential will require removal, the pin re-welding from underneath and the mountings boxed to prevent recurrence. A professional repair will cost circa ⬤x350.

Driveshaft wear

Ex | Gd | Av | Po
4 | 3 | 2 | 1

You may have checked the driveshafts while under the car, but driving can generate a 'click' which suggests a worn sliding joint in the rear driveshafts. A replacement shaft is required.

Universal joints

Ex | Gd | Av | Po
4 | 3 | 2 | 1

You may find that, collectively, the six u/js in the propeller shaft and driveshafts 'chunk'. While the new u/js are not expensive (six will cost £70), fitting will take some time if only because of the need to remove the differential.

Instruments/warning lights

Ex | Gd | Av | Po
4 | 3 | 2 | 1

This check is primarily to establish that they all work well. Neither the speedo nor tacho needles should waiver unduly. The ignition light should go out as engine revs build, and the oil pressure should not fade as water temperature increases. Take this opportunity to assess what the instruments tell you about the car: e.g. does the oil pressure suggest an engine in good or poor condition, does the water temperature rise steadily suggesting an ineffective radiator or an engine that is generating too much heat?

A thud from the rear of the car when the clutch is let out tells you this, and possibly three similar pins, have pulled out of the chassis.

The boxing operation complete.

There is a sliding spline in each rear driveshaft.

Switches

Ex 4 Gd 3 Av 2 Po 1

Check the switches that operate the heater fan (two speed), internal light, wipers (two speed) and screen washers. Check the turn indicator stork operates not only direction lights but the headlamp flash/dip/un-dip functions, too.

Brake servo

Ex 4 Gd 3 Av 2 Po 1

Before you finish the road test part of your examination, check that the servo is operating. Switch off the engine and place your foot on the brake pedal; you should hear a 'chuff' noise. Operate the brakes a couple of times and then, with your foot still on the pedal, restart the engine. You should feel the pedal depress if your servo is working satisfactorily. No 'chuff' and/or no depression and you should question the effectiveness of your servo.

Performance

Ex 4 Gd 3 Av 2 Po 1

How did the car go generally? Did the engine rev willingly up to, say, 4000rpm? Did it accelerate briskly and feel as if, in the right circumstances, it was a 100mph+ car? Did you spot any smoke from the exhaust – if so take a fresh look at the rear bumper and back panel where any serious exhaust fumes will have left deposits.

Exhaust smoke

Ex 4 Gd 3 Av 2 Po 1

As you get out of the car, leave the engine running and check that the exhaust is not puffing out smoke – black possibly signals a worn engine or very rich mixture, while white smoke could mean a blown head gasket. Remove the oil filler from the rocker cover and look at the oil covering inside. If thick and black the car may not have been maintained as you would wish; if emulsified/white you probably have a head gasket problem.

Mechanical aspects

Lift the bonnet/hood and check the following:

Wiring

Ex 4 Gd 3 Av 2 Po 1

The original wiring loom must not be chafed, but secured neatly to the shell using the tangs welded there. The exposed wires to the distributor, oil pressure and water temperature senders (which get hot, embrittling the PVC insulation) should not be cracked. Take a good look at all non-original (usually unwrapped) wires that may have been added by previous owners for security alarms, extra lights, etc. If they have secondary insulation, follow secure routes to their destination, use appropriate auto wires and colours, then

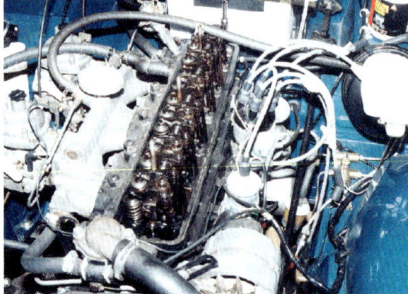

The electrical harness shown here has been installed perfectly.

all may be well. Amateur installations are often positivey dangerous to the car and should be viewed with scepticism.

Fuel pump wiring (petrol injected cars only)

Check that the power cable to and from the earth line for the fuel pump (in the boot/trunk) is heavy-duty cable. Early cars were under-cabled, resulting in a voltage drop to the pump which contributed to overheating.

Fuel lines

Ex 4 Gd 3 Av 2 Po 1

Check that the flexible fuel lines in the engine bay are in good order. This is applicable whether the car is petrol injected or not, but since there are numerous additional lines with a PI car, it becomes particularly important. Cracking, particularly with modern, aggressive unleaded fuels, is likely if the car has not had the rubber based fuel lines changed. If the car is running on carburettors, is the fuel filter clean (signifying it has been changed fairly recently)?

Radiator, hoses and fan

Ex 4 Gd 3 Av 2 Po 1

From the engine bay the radiator should look in good order with no evidence of weeping from the radiator itself (the giveaway is staining from the antifreeze), hoses, heater tap or head/block joint. Try to rotate the fan to check that the drive belt is driving on the sides of the 'vee' (worn belts partially drive on the flat base of the pulley for a short while). If the fan is electric, spin it to ensure it moves freely. Only give excellent marks to a car in good order with a well installed electric fan.

Battery

Ex 4 Gd 3 Av 2 Po 1

These days a battery can be easily replaced but its condition may tell you a bit not only about the battery itself but also the care that the car has received. A new battery with pristine terminations can be given top marks, but look for white powder forming round the terminal posts (poor marks) and dry connections to the positive and negative posts (average).

Washer bottle

Ex 4 Gd 3 Av 2 Po 1

The washer bottle should be in good order, be retained to its carrier by a flexible band, and work!

Engine oil leaks

Ex 4 Gd 3 Av 2 Po 1

Obviously, you need to inspect right around the engine from

Ex 4 Gd 3 Av 2 Po 1

Just forward of the wiper motor is the fuel pump relay, and the place to check whether the wires to the fuel pump are of adequate gauge.

The six fuel lines that pass over the rocker cover need to be in first class order.

This refurbished PI TR6 sets the standard you seek for cooling duct, radiator and reinforced top hose.

the engine bay, but the most likely oil leak is from the back of the rocker cover – where I bet you see a trail down onto the top of the bellhousing. This is most likely the result of the original pressed steel rocker cover being over-tightened and distorted. Only award excellent marks if an aftermarket polished cast cover has been fitted and is not leaking.

Engine mountings

Look down both sides of the engine at the flexible rubber engine mountings. Check whether they are cracked and if in doubt, start the engine and recheck with the engine running.

The pressed rocker cover is very susceptible to oil leaks just in front of the battery.

Carbs and linkages (carburettor only)

This is an important check point, particularly if you think the car is running poorly. First, check for any fuel leaks. Secondly, turn the throttle to as far open as you can and try moving the throttle spindle on each carburettor up and down and in and out. There should be no discernible 'flop', but wear in one or both throttle spindles will need to be corrected before the car will run as intended. Check the choke operates and that the inter-carb linkages are sound and secure.

The later CF 'swept' inlet manifold.

Inlet manifold (carburettor only)

There are several types of inlet manifold. Mark as indicated:

Poor – a US CC model with an original cylinder head and associated inlet manifold.

Average – a CC model with UK cylinder head and associated inlet manifold (this has the advantage of being compatible with the numerous tuning equipment available).

Good – a later CF swept inlet manifold, seen above.

A professional Bosch PI fuel pump and filter is ideal when installed in the spare wheel well.

Fuel pump (petrol injection only)

If the car is fitted with an original Lucas PI pump and filter (located in the boot/trunk), award average marks, provided your test drive did not reveal any problems. If the car has been fitted with a Bosch fuel pump by the owner, mark it as good, but if you can be shown that the Bosch fuel pump and filter assembly were supplied and fitted by a reputable TR specialist, give this section excellent marks.

Exhaust manifold/header

A TR6 will perform better if an aftermarket tubular exhaust has replaced the original cast iron version. So mark:

Average – original cast iron.
Good – mild steel tubular.
Excellent – stainless steel tubular.

Unleaded fuel conversion (all cars)

Ask to see proof that the cylinder head has been converted to use unleaded fuel. This involves machining away the original valve seats and replacing them with hardened inserts, new valves and phosphor bronze valve guides.

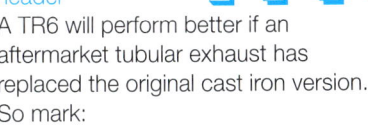

The original cast exhaust manifold and a pair of Stromberg 175 carburettors.

Unleaded fuel conversion (petrol injection only check)

The PI metering unit was designed long before modern day unleaded fuels were formulated, and, sadly, today's fuels create problems with the shuttle and seals in a PI fuel distribution system. Therefore, mark the section poor if the car is fitted with an original metering unit and excellent if you can be shown an invoice from a reputable TR specialist for fitting an unleaded/re-calibrated metering unit.

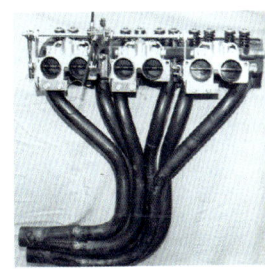

The more effective tubular mild steel upgrade.

Engine and chassis number check

While you've got your head in the engine bay, write down the engine number and chassis/commission number so that you can check it with the vendor's documentation later.

Crankshaft endfloat

We checked for the characteristic thudding when seated in the cockpit (p29), but now, while you are 'in' the engine bay with the engine off, check the fore-aft movement of the crankshaft. Push the front pulley as far back as possible then have the vendor push the clutch to the floor while you feel/measure the forward movement of the

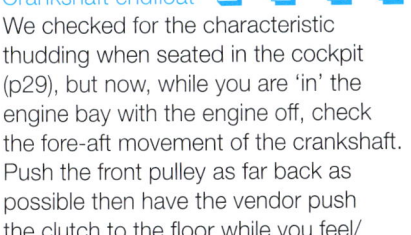

The metering unit – you will be seeking a receipt proving the one fitted to your PI car is suitable for use with unleaded fuel.

front pulley. There should be no discernible movement. If there is over 1.5mm float

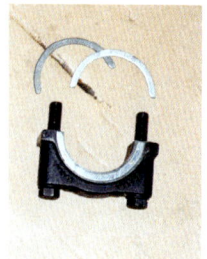

then the crankshaft thrust bearings are excessively worn and must at least be replaced, though ideally upgraded using the improved bearing shown above.

The fan/drive belt loops round the front pulley where you will test the crankshaft endfloat.

Aesthetics

You should not buy or reject a car on the basis of its hood, carpets and internal lining panels. A poor car beautifully trimmed is not a good buy while. conversely, a sound car with tatty trim is worth purchasing at the right price.

Hood frame

Is the hood frame present; does it go up and down (fairly) easily; is it in good (re-painted) condition or rusted?

A particularly nice example of the hood frame ...

Hood and cover

Is the hood in good condition? Is it in the right colour? Are there tears, splits or cracks in the hood material or the rear windows? Is it taut or loose? Is the main rear window crystal-clear, creased/slightly opaque, rather scratched or useless

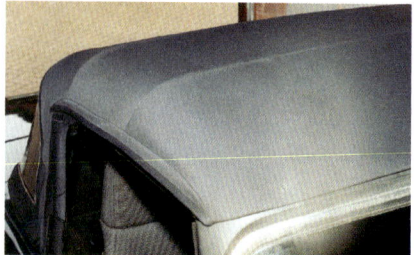

... and a nice taut hood in mohair material.

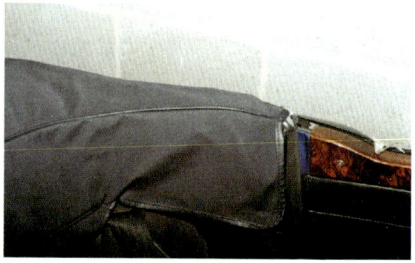

A tonneau cover can substitute for the hood cover we see here.

by virtue of clouding? Is a hood or a tonneau cover supplied? If a tonneau, does the tonneau zip slide easily its full length?

Dashboard and trim

Ex	Gd	Av	Po
4	3	2	1

Are all the correct instruments in place and matching. The picture shows a mixture of early and late small dials, which warrants a substantial markdown. Original CP/CC cars have hanging needles in the small dials and black bezels. CR/CF small instrument needles should point up and all dials have a slightly different font and part-chromed bezels (see also page13).

Cockpit carpets

Ex	Gd	Av	Po
4	3	2	1

The carpets are fairly quickly replaced but nevertheless should be in mint condition to attract an excellent mark. Are the footwell carpets stuck to the floor (they must be removable)? Does the car have sound-deadening felt? Are the felts stuck to the floor or the underside of the carpet (mark down if stuck to the floor)? Are supplementary floor mats fitted?

Steering wheel

Ex	Gd	Av	Po
4	3	2	1

Is the original steering wheel on the car, or, if an aftermarket wheel, is the original TR6 wheel supplied with the car (they are now in short supply)? If so, is it in good condition?

Seats and runners

Ex	Gd	Av	Po
4	3	2	1

Are all four seat covers (two per seat) in good condition? Do the seat adjustments work well, and do the seat runners look in good order (they can rust badly)?

Trim panels

Ex	Gd	Av	Po
4	3	2	1

The TR6 is trimmed internally by a number

The instruments (in this case the later CR/CF model with vertical needles in small gauges), veneer and some of the crash padding ...

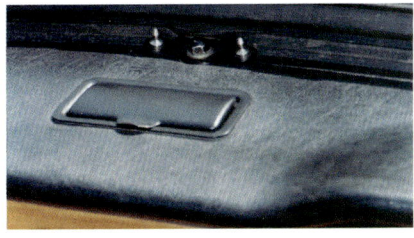

... while this is the top padding.

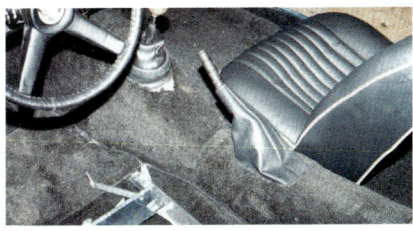

A very nice carpet set establishes an excellent standard ...

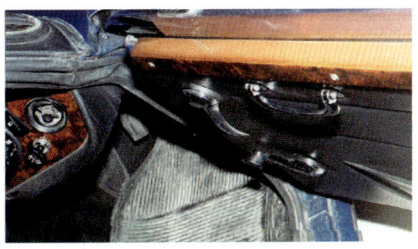

... as does this vinyl door panel and non-standard veneered top trim.

of vinyl-covered panels, by far the most important of which are the door panels. Are all the trim panels in place and in acceptable condition? Do the door panels look as if they have suffered water damage from inside the door? Are all the door fittings/furniture in place and in good order?

A concours standard rear on an early CP model without the usual black rear panel.

Glass, front and sides

Ex. Gd. Av. Po
4 3 2 1

Is the windscreen/windshield free from stone chips or wiper scratches? What about scratches on the side glasses, particularly on the driver's side, and chips from the top of the door windows?

Exterior trim/bumpers

Ex. Gd. Av. Po
4 3 2 1

If you are seeking a top quality car, look at the external brightwork with a critical eye. The replacement front bumpers in particular are usually not up to the standard of the original item so good original bumpers will be important to potential concours entrants. The chrome finish can be replaced (at some expense) but holed, accident-damaged and bent bumpers present a problem and should be marked severely.

Standard 5½J wheels with non-standard oversized tyres for additional road-holding but slightly heavier steering. This car is in fact very non-standard, in that it has been fitted with a V8 engine.

Wheels and wheel condition

The TR6 was originally fitted with 5½ J 15in diameter steel wheels but later cars had the (preferable) 6J wide wheels. Time usually rusts steel wheels so check at least the outer faces for corrosion and mark even higher (unless you plan concours competition) if a set of alloy (ideally 5!) wheels have been fitted.

Tyre condition

Needless to say the condition of the tyres has important safety implications, so check the full-width tread on the road wheels, their make (never heard of them or a well-known brand?) and side wall appearance. Mark very cautiously, particularly if side wall cracking/crazing, a consequence of longevity, is evident.

Door locks/keys

Check the keys are available, whether there is a duplicate set, that both door locks work off the same key, and that the boot/trunk and glove pocket locks perform.

In the boot/trunk

The boot/trunk trim was never luxurious but should be present, hiding the tank and the rear wings/fenders. A spare wheel and roadworthy tyre should reside under a removable floor, and a jack/wheel brace and some basic tools should be available.

Roadworthiness test certificate

In the UK we would call it an MoT certificate, Germany uses the term TUV or DEKRA for a similar test, France calls it a Contrôle Technique, while in the USA individual states set their own test requirements. France even makes it illegal to sell a vehicle without a recent CT certificate. However, you need to see the most recent roadworthiness (and where applicable, emissions) certification for the car and mark this section according to the remaining period of validity.

Evaluation procedure

Add up the total points scored.

Petrol injected: 384 points = first class, possibly concours; **288 points** = good/very good; **192 points** = average; **96 points** = poor.

Carburettor: 388 points = first class, possibly concours; **291 points** = good/very good; **194 points** = average; **97 points** = poor.

Cars scoring over 270 should be completely usable and require the minimum of repair, although continued maintenance and care will be required to keep them in condition. Cars scoring between 96 and 197 points will require a full restoration – the cost of which will be much the same regardless of points scored. Cars scoring between 198 and 270 points will require very careful assessment of the necessary repair/restoration costs in order to arrive at a realistic purchase value.

10 Auctions
– sold! Another way to buy your dream

Pros: Auctions operate as trade rather than retail markets, so prices are often lower than those on dealer premises and from some private sellers. Auctioneers have usually confirmed ownership title with the seller, and it should be possible to check this and any other relevant paperwork. You may also receive 24 hours of warranty cover.

Cons: You may get only minimal information before travelling to the venue, or vague and sometimes very sales-orientated descriptions. To avoid disappointment, learn to read between the lines of the catalogue or website description, and only visit if there are several candidate cars. Star lots may be stored indoors under good light, but there is limited scope to examine the cars thoroughly. The wise buyer gets to the venue early and would do well to take this book, a mirror and a torch. Classic cars cannot be road tested, so for nearby venues try to arrive early on any preview days to see the lots arriving and being off-loaded or marshalled into position. The attendants may also be prepared to start a car for you. Intended as trade sales, the cars often need valeting, which dealers are happy to do and should not put you off.

Do your research, decide your personal limit and stick to it. Remember the auctioneer's charges, or the extra 5-10% may come as a shock. Admission is normally by catalogue and usually covers two people, so take a friend; it's amazing what a second pair of eyes can spot.

Catalogue prices and payment details

Auction catalogues and websites normally feature an estimated price and will spell out all charges and acceptable payment methods. Be sure you can comply before bidding. An immediate part-payment or deposit is usually requested if you win, with the balance payable within 24 hours. Check for cash and credit card limits, and personal cheques, debit card or banker's draft options. The car won't be released until all costs are cleared, with storage normally at your expense.

Viewing

It may be possible to view in the day/hours before an auction. Staff or owners may unlock doors, engine and luggage compartments for inspection, or start the engine. Examining the car is fine but you may not jack it up, so take a mirror on a stick.

eBay & other online auctions

eBay and other online auctions could land you a car at a bargain price, though you'd be foolhardy to bid without examining it first. A useful feature of eBay is that the location of the car is shown, so you can narrow your choices. Be prepared to be outbid in the last few moments of the auction. Remember, your bid is binding, and it will be very, very difficult to get restitution in the case of a crooked seller fleecing you – caveat emptor!

Note that some cars offered for sale online are 'ghost' cars. Don't part with any cash without being sure the vehicle actually exists and is as described.

11 Paperwork
– correct documentation is essential!

The paper trail

Classic, collector and prestige cars usually come with a large portfolio of paperwork, accumulated and passed on by a succession of proud owners. This documentation represents the real history of the car and from it can be deduced the level of care the car has received, how much it's been used, which specialists have worked on it, and the dates of major repairs and restorations. All of this information will be priceless to you as the new owner, so be very wary of cars with little paperwork to support their claimed history.

Registration documents

All countries/states have some form of registration for private vehicles, whether it's like the American 'pink slip' system or the British 'log book' system.

It is essential to check that the registration document is genuine, that it relates to the car in question, and that all the vehicle's details are correctly recorded, including chassis/VIN and engine numbers (if these are shown). If you are buying from the previous owner, his or her name and address will be recorded in the document: this will not be the case if you are buying from a dealer.

In the UK the current (EU-aligned) registration document is named V5C, and is printed in coloured sections of blue, green and pink. The blue section relates to the car specification, the green section has details of the new owner and the pink section is sent to the DVLA in the UK when the car is sold. A small section in yellow deals with selling the car within the motor trade.

In the UK the DVLA will provide details of earlier keepers of the vehicle upon payment of a small fee, and much can be learned in this way.

If the car has a foreign registration there may be expensive and time-consuming formalities to complete. Do you really want the hassle?

Roadworthiness certificate

Most country/state administrations require that vehicles are regularly tested to prove they are safe to use on the public highway and do not produce excessive emissions. In the UK that test (the MoT) is carried out at approved testing stations, for a fee. In the USA the requirement varies, but most states insist on an emissions test every two years as a minimum, while the police are charged with pulling over unsafe-looking vehicles.

In the UK the test is required on an annual basis once a vehicle becomes three years old. Of particular relevance for older cars is that the certificate issued includes the mileage reading recorded at the test date and, therefore, becomes an independent record of that car's history. Ask the seller if previous certificates are available. Without an MoT the vehicle should be trailered to its new home, unless you insist that a valid MoT is part of the deal. (Not such a bad idea, this, as at least you will know the car was roadworthy on the day it was tested and you don't need to wait for the old certificate to expire before having the test done.)

Road licence

The administration of every country/state charges some kind of tax for the use of its road system, the actual form of the 'road licence', and how it is displayed, varying enormously country-to-country and state-to-state.

Whatever the form of the 'road licence', it must relate to the vehicle carrying it and must be present and valid if the car is to be driven legally on the public highway. The value of the license will depend on the length of time it will be valid.

In the UK if a car is untaxed because it has not been used for a period of time, the owner has to inform the licencing authorities, otherwise the vehicle's date-related registration number will be lost and there will be a painful amount of paperwork to get it re-registered. Also in the UK, vehicles built before the end of 1972 are provided with tax discs free of charge, which must still be displayed. Car clubs can often provide formal proof that a particular car qualifies for this valuable concession.

Certificates of authenticity

For many makes of collectible car it is possible to get a certificate proving the age and authenticity (e.g. engine and chassis numbers, paint colour and trim) of a particular vehicle; these are sometimes called 'Heritage certificates' and if the car comes with one it is a definite bonus. If you want to obtain a certificate, the relevant owners club is the best starting point.

If the car has been used in European classic car rallies it may have a FIVA (Federation Internationale des Vehicules Anciens) certificate. The so-called 'FIVA Passport', or 'FIVA Vehicle Identity Card,' enables organisers and participants to recognise whether or not a particular vehicle is suitable for individual events. If you want to obtain such a certificate go to www.fbhvc.co.uk or www.fiva.org. There will be similar organisations in other countries, too.

Valuation certificate

Hopefully, the vendor will have a recent valuation certificate, or letter signed by a recognised expert, stating how much he, or she, believes the particular car to be worth (such documents, together with photos, are usually needed to get 'agreed value' insurance). Generally, such documents should act only as confirmation of your own assessment of the car rather than a guarantee of value as the expert has probably not seen the car in the flesh. The easiest way to find out how to obtain a formal valuation is to contact one of the specialist suppliers listed in Chapter 16.

Service history

Often these cars will have been serviced at home by enthusiastic (and hopefully capable) owners for a good number of years. Nevertheless, try to obtain as much service history and other paperwork pertaining to the car as you can. Naturally, dealer stamps, or specialist garage receipts, score most points in the value stakes. However, anything helps in the great authenticity game, items like the original bill of sale, handbook, parts invoices, and repair bills all adding to the story and character of the car. Even a brochure correct to the year of the car's manufacture is a useful document and something that you could well have to search hard to locate in future years. If the seller claims that the car has been restored, then expect receipts and other evidence from a specialist restorer.

If the seller claims to have carried out regular servicing, ask what work was completed, when, and seek some evidence of it being done. Your assessment of the car's overall condition should tell you whether the seller's claims are genuine.

Restoration photographs

If the seller tells you that the car has been restored, expect to be shown a series of photographs taken while the restoration was under way. Pictures taken at various stages, and from various angles, should help you gauge the thoroughness of the work. If you buy the car, ask if you can have all the photographs as they form an important part of the vehicle's history. It's surprising how many sellers are happy to part with their car and accept your cash, but want to hang on to their photographs! In the latter event, you may be able to persuade the vendor to get a set of copies made.

12 What's it worth to you?
– let your head rule your heart!

Condition

If the car you've been looking at is really bad, then you've probably not used the marking system in Chapter 9 (60 minute evaluation). If you did use the marking system, you'll know whether the car is in excellent (maybe concours), good, average or poor condition.

Many classic/collector car magazines run a regular price guide. If you haven't bought the latest issues, do so now and compare their suggested values for the model you are thinking of buying, and look at the auction prices they're reporting. Values have been fairly stable for some time, but some models will always be more sought-after than others. Trends can change, too. The values in the magazines tend to vary from one publication to another, as do scales of condition, so read carefully the guidance notes they provide. Bear in mind that a car which is truly a recent show winner could be worth more than the highest scale published. Assuming that the car you have in mind is not in show/concours condition, relate the level of condition that you judge the car to be in to the appropriate guide price. How does the figure compare with the asking price? Before you start haggling with the seller, consider what affect any variation from standard specification might have on the value.

If you are buying from a dealer, remember there will be a premium within the price.

Desirable options/extras

Petrol injection cars are the most sought-after
Overdrive on gearbox
Clutch thrust fork securing upgrade
CF/CR or reinforced earlier chassis
Crankshaft thrust bearing upgrade
Telescopic rear damper conversion
Polyurethane rear suspension bushes
Electric fan conversion
Oil cooler conversion
Spin-on oil filter conversion
Tubular exhaust manifolds and sports exhaust system
Electronic ignition conversion
Bosch fuel pump conversion on PI cars
Weber carburettor conversion on carburettor induction cars
6J alloy wheels with wider-section tyres (up to 195 x 65 x 15)
6J 72-spoke heavy-duty wire wheels
Upgraded front brakes
Mohair hood
Separate headrests/head restraints built atop the seats

Undesirable features

Non-original colour
Original, but out of the ordinary paintwork
Fibreglass body panels
Large rubber over-riders on the bumpers
Originality enthusiasts would prefer an original steering wheel to an aftermarket one (my TR6 has an aftermarket wheel).

Striking a deal

Negotiate on the basis of your condition assessment, mileage, and fault correction cost. Also take into account the specification. Be realistic about the value, but don't be completely intractable – a small compromise on the part of the vendor or buyer will often facilitate a deal at little real cost to either.

13 Do you really want to restore?
– it'll take longer and cost more than you think

There is a lot going for any practical enthusiast who wants to restore a TR6. Firstly, everything comes apart, which makes access much easier than with many other classic cars. Secondly, the 'fit' of the replacement body panels is generally quite good, which means you do not need years of body repair experience to tackle a TR6 body restoration. Parts availability is excellent, and the car is basically a simple vehicle that enables many enthusiasts from all walks of life to carry out superb restorations. Perhaps the deciding factor for many is that, with a TR6, if you do the majority of work yourself, you will be pretty sure to recoup most of your expenditure.

So, restoring a TR6 is not impractical by any means. Nevertheless, it is a sad but inescapable fact that all too frequently owners fail to complete restoration projects. Often the incomplete car then becomes an 'abandoned project' entry in the 'For sale' columns. Furthermore, in these circumstances, rarely does the owner recover his costs. One reason for this is that the car appears to want nothing much more than a little care and attention – but things are ALWAYS worse, usually far worse, than the unsuspecting owner ever imagined. He removes a wing/fender and finds tin worm everywhere – whereupon things go progressively downhill. One car I bought in thousands of pieces had started about five years previously with a slipping clutch. Out came the engine and gearbox but both revealed unexpected wear and were stripped for rectification. Frankly, I am not sure how this progressed to starter and wiper motors, front wings and even the sills/rockers, but the car ended up in dozens of boxes and quite beyond the owner's capability to repair and reassemble it. Ask yourself whether you have the technical competence to undertake a full restoration and the will to seek help if things get out of hand.

You also need to ask yourself whether you have the money to finance professional help. Probably the single most frequent reason for incomplete restoration projects is that the costs proved more than was initially envisaged, followed fairly closely by the work taking far longer than was expected. Even for the experienced, the costs and timescales are ALWAYS more than expected!

The technical, cost and time issues are largely trade-offs. The more technically competent you are, the more you can do yourself. The more you can do yourself the less the project should cost but the longer it will take.

Mind you, there are other reasons that projects become abandoned: insufficient space, tools, and workshop facilities are all contributory factors. Do you appreciate that a disassembled TR6 takes up about triple the space of an assembled one? What about the welding set, benders, hand tools, lighting, heating, and location where you can bash away in the evening without the neighbours and/or partner getting upset?

Even before you buy a 'restoration project' car, prepare for and plan the restoration very carefully. Most people only carry out one restoration in their lives so look through Chapter 16 and seek advice from club members who have done it, read the relevant books, and talk to the professionals before you start. Where something can be postponed for a year or two (e.g. an engine rebuild), do so. Where you have to get the whole job done thoroughly first time (e.g. body panel repairs and paint spraying) be sure you do so even if it means using professionals for that part of the project.

The body is probably the first part of most TR6 restorations and is probably the most difficult task for many enthusiasts. This would be typical of the sort of cutting required to get back to the solid metal that must be your starting point. There will then be a lot of paint to apply before the body is finished.

After you have finished restoring the body you'll need to lift it clear of the chassis and mechanical parts. Can you face finding this beneath? Actually, compared to some, this rolling chassis looks quite good!

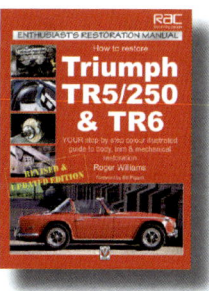

ISBN: 978-1-903706-46-6

After stripping the mechanical components from the chassis, you will need to repair the inevitable chassis rot, after which address the mechanical refurbishment before refitting the body to the chassis. Fortunately, help is available in a detailed book published by Veloce but, nevertheless, a TR6 restoration is no quick job.

14 Paint problems

– a bad complexion, including dimples, pimples and bubbles

Paint faults generally occur due to lack of protection/maintenance, or poor preparation prior to a respray or touch-up. Some of the following conditions may be present in the car you're looking at:

Orange peel

This appears as an uneven paint surface, similar in appearance to the skin of an orange, hence the name. The fault is caused by the failure of atomized paint droplets to flow into each other when they hit the surface. It's sometimes possible to eraset the effect with proprietary paint cutting/rubbing compound or very fine grades of abrasive paper. A respray may be necessary in severe cases. Consult a bodywork repairer/paint shop for advice on the particular car.

Orange peel.

Cracking

Severe cases are likely to have been caused by too heavy an application of paint (or filler beneath the paint). Also, insufficient stirring of the paint before application can result in components being improperly mixed, and cracking can result. Incompatibility with the paint already on the panel can have a similar effect. To rectify the problem it is necessary to rub down to a smooth, sound finish before respraying the problem area.

Crazing

Sometimes the paint takes on a crazed rather than a cracked appearance when the problems mentioned under 'Cracking' are present. This problem can also be caused by a reaction between the underlying surface and the paint. Paint removal and respraying the problem area is usually the only solution.

Blistering

Almost always caused by corrosion of the metal beneath the paint. Usually perforation will be found in the metal and the damage will be worse than that suggested by the area of blistering. The metal will have to be repaired before repainting.

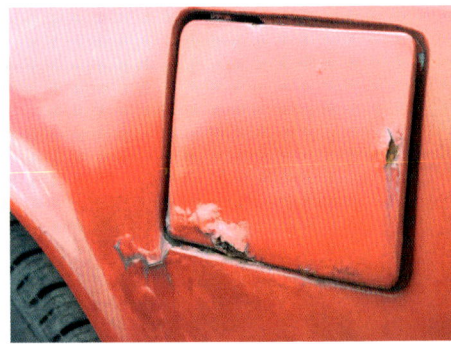

Rust blistering.

Micro blistering

Usually the result of an economy respray where inadequate heating has allowed moisture to settle on the car before spraying. Consult a paint specialist, but usually damaged paint will have to be removed before partial or full respraying. Can also be caused by car covers that don't 'breathe'.

Fading

Some colours, especially reds, are prone to fading if subjected to strong sunlight for long periods without the benefit of polish protection. Sometimes proprietary paint restorers and/or paint cutting/rubbing compounds will retrieve the situation. Often a respray is the only real solution.

Peeling

Often a problem with metallic paintwork when the sealing laquer becomes damaged and begins to peel off. Poorly applied paint may also peel. The remedy is to strip and start again!

Dimples

Dimples in the paintwork are caused by polish residue (particularly silicone types) not being properly removed before respraying. Paint removal and repainting is the only solution.

Dents

Small dents are usually easily cured by the 'Dentmaster', or equivalent process, that sucks or pushes out the dent (as long as the paint surface is still intact). Companies offering dent removal services usually come to your home: consult your telephone directory.

Dimples and orange peel.

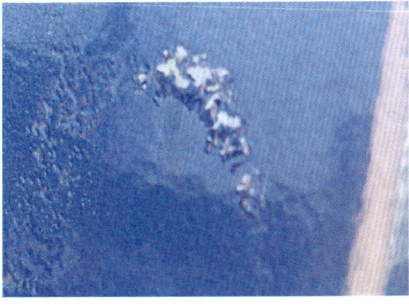

Reaction and rust blistering.

15 Problems due to lack of use

– just like their owners, cars need exercise!

A run of at least ten miles, once a week, is recommended for classics if conditions are dry and the car is taxed, insured and roadworthy. If an actual run is impractical I suggest you start and use as many of its systems as possible for fifteen to twenty minutes once a month. This is particularly valuable if you have the rear wheels safely up on axle stands and can thus exercise the clutch, gearbox, overdrive, rear axle and brakes. Ensure the engine is used for long enough to open the thermostat, whereupon you should circulate the coolant with some vigour (i.e. do not leave the car idling) for a minimum of five minutes. I like 2500rpm for these warm-ups.

Check and inflate the tyres to running pressure. I would also disconnect the earth/ground terminal from the battery until it's time for another start-up, but connect a battery conditioner or trickle charger for a few hours after the periodic exercise. Never leave the car unused with:

• The hand/parking brake on, as the shoes can rust to the drums and the cable seize/freeze.

• The weight of the car on the tyres. An unchanged position develops flat spots, resulting in (sometimes temporary) vibration. Furthermore, the tyre walls may crack or develop blister-type bulges, necessitating new tyres.

• Weak or no antifreeze protection in the coolant. The corrosion inhibitors in antifreeze help prevent corroded internal waterways and, of course, stop freezing which can cause core plugs to be pushed out and even cracks in the block or head. Silt settling and solidifying can cause subsequent overheating.

• Old/well-used engine oil in the sump/oil pan. The acid that builds up during combustion corrodes bearings.

When you are looking at potential purchases, bear in mind that, after long periods of inactivity, the following problems are also likely, depending on the period of inactivity, storage conditions, and pre-storage preparation:

Seized components

• Pistons can seize in the engine cylinders due to corrosion.

• Pistons in brake and clutch calipers, slave and master cylinders can seize.

• The bonnet/hood cable and catch can seize/freeze.

• The clutch may seize if the plate becomes stuck to the flywheel because of corrosion.

• Lip seals in the main working components stick to their respective shafts and can be damaged upon starting.

• Brake fluid absorbs water from the atmosphere and should be renewed every two years. However, in storage conditions old fluid with a high water content can

If you bought a car with an engine bay looking like this you would expect the engine to be seized/frozen. To free a seized engine remove the plugs and fill each bore with diesel fuel for a week or two, then (hopefully) blow out what's left through the plug holes. Be sure to change the oil afterwards.

cause corrosion within the braking system, and pistons/calipers to seize/freeze. This, in turn, can cause brake failure when the water turns to vapour near to hot braking components.

● With lack of use, the shock absorbers/dampers will lose elasticity, or even seize. Creaking, groaning and stiff suspension are signs of this problem.

● Radiator hoses may have perished and split, possibly resulting in the loss of all coolant. Window and door seals can harden and leak. Gaitors/boots can crack. Wiper blades will harden.

● The battery will be of little use if it has not been charged for many months. Earthing/grounding problems are common when the connections have corroded. Old bullet-and-spade type electrical connectors commonly rust or corrode and will require disconnecting, cleaning and protection (e.g. Vaseline). Sparkplug electrodes will often have corroded in an unused engine. Wiring insulation can harden and fail.

● Mild steel exhaust systems corrode when a car is unused as the result of high water content and combustion gasses trapped in the system. Expect non-stainless systems to need replacing as part of your re-commissioning costs.

You know you are in trouble when you remove the brake master cylinder top and see ... nothing. Although it is inevitable that the master cylinder – and probably the calipers and rear slave cylinders – will be seized, they should never be thrown away, as new replacement hydraulic components are becoming very scarce. You may even find you need a part exchange component if you are to buy a refurbished replacement. Today, specialist companies bore and sleeve even seized master cylinders like this to keep a steady supply of hydraulic components available.

A seized/frozen bonnet/hood catch doesn't sound too serious, but on a TR6 it presents an interesting problem, as access on the bulkhead/firewall in front of the screen is very restricted. If storing a TR6, leave the bonnet/hood unlatched and grease/exercise the catch via its cable as often as you can. This catch has been fitted with two release cables.

The overdrive cross shaft (arrow 1) can seize/freeze both in storage and in use. This picture shows two additional gearbox details mentioned elsewhere. Arrow 2 focuses on the clutch actuating folk that can break, while arrow 3 points out the middle of three holes where the TR6 clutch should connect.

16 The Community

– key people, organisations and companies in the TR6 world

Clubs

The Triumph TR6 & 250 Club of America ('6-PACK'), PO Box 30064, Cincinnati, OH 45230, USA.
E-mail: membership@6-pack.org
www.6-pack.org

TR Drivers Club, 17 Burgundy Close, Locksheath, Southampton, Hants, SO81 6PS, England. Tel 01562 825000.
E-mail: trdriver@btinternet.com

TR Register, 1B Hawkesworth, Southmead Industrial Park, Didcot, Oxon, OX11 7HR, England. Tel 01235 818866.
E-mail: tr.register@onyxnet.co.uk.
www.tr-register.co.uk

Vintage Triumph Register, 15218 West Warren Avenue, Dearborn, MI 48126, USA. E-mail: vtr-www@www.vtr.org
www.vtr.org

UK main restorers, repairers, dealers and spares suppliers

Revington TR, Home Farm, Middlezoy, Somerset, TA7 0PD, England. Tel 01823 698437. Email info@revingtontr.com
www.revingtontr.com

Rimmer Bros, Sleaford Road, Bracebridge Heath, Lincoln, LN4 2NA England. Tel 01522 568000.
E-mail: sales@rimmerbros.co.uk

TR Bitz, Lyncastle Way, Barley Castle Trading Estate, Appleton Thorn, Warrington, Cheshire, WA4 4ST England. Tel 01925 861861.
E-mail: triumph@trbitz.u-net.com

This is a typical TR Register meeting in the UK where like-minded enthusiasts meet for socialising, fun and friendly competition.

TR Enterprises, Dale Lane, Blidworth, Mansfield, Nottinghamshire, NG21 0SA England. Tel 01623 793807.
E-mail: stevehall@trenterprises.com

TRGB Ltd, Unit 1 Sycamore Farm Industrial Estate, Long Drove, Somersham, Huntingdon, Cambs, PE17 3HJ, England. Tel 01487 842168.
www.trgb.co.uk

UK main spares suppliers

Moss-Europe, Hampton Farm Estate, Hanworth, Middlesex, TW13 6DB, England. Tel 020 88672020.
E-mail: sales@moss-europe.co.uk

US main spares suppliers

The Roadster Factory, PO Box 332, Killen Road, Armagh, PA 15920, USA. Tel (800) 678-8764.
www.the-roadster-factory.com

Moss Motors, PO Box 847, 440 Rutherford Street, Goleta, CA 93116, USA. Tel (800) 667-7872.
www.mossmotors.com

Victoria British Ltd. Box 14991, Lenexa, KS 66285-4991, USA. Tel (800) 255-0088. www.longmotor.com

Overdrive repair specialists

Overdrive Repair Services, Units C3/4 Ellisons Road, Norwood Industrial Estate, Killamarsh, Sheffield, S21 2JG England. Tel 0114 2482632. www.overdrive-repairs.co.uk/products

Overdrive spares, Unit A2 Wolston Business Park, Main Street, Wolston, Nr Coventry, CV8 3FU. England. Tel 02476 543686. E-mail: odspares@aol.com

Gearbox rebuilding

First Gear, 3 Church View, Beckingham, Doncaster, DN10 4PD, England. Tel 01427 848101.

Chassis repair and manufacture

CTM Engineering, Unit 3A, Bury Farm, Curbridge, Nr Botley, Hants SO30 2HB, England. Tel 01489 782054. E-mail: colin@ctmeng.freeserve.co.uk

Electrical

TR250/6 Maintenance Handbook by Dan Masters. Available from DMP, PO Box 6430, Maryville, TN 37802-6430 USA. $30 surface/$36 air mail. http://members.aol.com/danmas6/

PI specialists

Prestige Developments & Injection, 77 Box Lane, Wrexham, Clwyd LL12 8DA, Wales. Tel 01978 263449. www.prestigeinjection.fsnet.co.uk

Brakes specialists

Hi Spec Motorsport, Unit 5 Parker Ind Centre, Watling St, Dartford Kent, DA2 6EP, England. Tel 01322 286850. www.hispecmotorsport.co.uk

Rally Design, Units 8-10, Upper Brents Ind Est, Faversham, Kent, ME13 7DZ, England. Tel 01795 531871. www.raddes.co.uk

Books

Triumph TR6 by William Kimberley – ISBN 1-901295-20-6. Veloce.
How to Restore Triumph TR5/250 &TR6 by Roger Williams
– ISBN 1-901295-92-3. Veloce.
How to Improve Triumph TR5, 250 & 6 by Roger Williams
– ISBN 1-903706-68-8. Veloce.
Original Triumph TR4/5/6 by Bill Piggott
– ISBN 1-901432-04-1.

Auctioneers

Barrett-Jackson
www.barrett-jackson.com
Bonhams
www.bonhams.com
British Car Auctions (BCA)
www.bca-europe.com
www.british-car-auctions.co.uk
Cheffins
www.cheffins.co.uk
Christies
www.christies.com
Coys
www.coys.co.uk
eBay
www.ebay.com
H&H
www.classic-auctions.co.uk
RM
www.rmauctions.com
Shannons
www.shannons.com.au
Silver
www.silverauctions.com

17 Vital statistics
– essential data at your fingertips

Common details

Engine – water-cooled 2498cc/152cu in OHV six-in-line cylinders. Iron block and head. Bore 74.7mm, stroke 95mm

Engine numbers use the chassis prefix

Brakes – Dual line close-coupled servo operating front discs, rear drums.

Handbrake operates on rear drums

Electrics – 12v battery, 12v coil and distributor, alternator

Kerb weight (including fluids but no driver) – 1085kg/2387lb

TR6 PI CP 150bhp model

Dates – November 1968 - October 1972

Chassis numbers – CP25001 (pre-production unit) – CP26998 ('69) + CP50001 – CP54572 ('70) + CP54717 – CP 54719 ('71) + CP 75001 – CP77718 ('72)

Number built – 9196 including 2808 assembled from CKD kits in Belgium

Performance – 142bhp net at 5500rpm, max torque 159lb/ft net at 3000rpm, max speed 117mph

0-60mph – 8.5sec according to *Motor,* June 1969

Induction – Lucas mechanical petrol injection

Transmission – 'A' type four-speed manual gearbox. Synchromesh on all forward gears. Some cars were fitted with 'A' type overdrive units operating on top three gears

Ignition key fitted to and actuated a steering column lock from CP50001.

TR6 CC model

Dates – November 1968 - October 1972

Chassis numbers – CC25001L (pre-production prototype) – CC32143L ('69) + CC50001L – CC67893L ('70/71) + CC75001L – CC85737U ('72)

Number built – 35774

Performance – max power 104bhp at 4500rpm, max torque 143lb/ft at 3000rpm, max speed 110mph

0-60mph – 9.8sec (*Car & Driver,* Feb 1969)

Induction – Twin side-draft Stromberg 175 1¾in carburettors

Transmission – 'A' type four-speed manual gearbox. Synchromesh on all forward gears. Some cars were fitted with 'A' type overdrive units operating on top three gears

Ignition key fitted to and actuated a steering column lock from CC50001L.

TR6 PI CR (Colloquially called '125bhp') model

Dates – October 1972 - February 1975

Chassis numbers – CR169 – CR2911 ('73) + CR5049 – CR6701 ('73/74/75)

Number built – 4564 including 792 assembled from CKD kits in Belgium

Performance –124bhp SAE at 5000rpm, max torque 146lb/ft SAE at 3500rpm, max speed 116mph

0-60mph – 9.5sec

Induction – Lucas mechanical petrol injection

Transmission – 'J' type four-speed manual gearbox. Synchromesh fitted to all forward gears. Some cars were fitted with 'J' type overdrive units operating on top two gears

Ignition key fitted to and actuated a steering column lock.

TR6 CF model

Dates – October 1972 - July 1976

Chassis numbers – CF1U – CF11577U (1973) + CF12501 – CF25777U ('74) + CF27002U – CF31533 ('74½)+ CF35002 – CF39991U ('75) + CF50001U – CF58328U ('76)

Number built – 42580

Performance – 101bhp at 4900rpm, max torque 128lb/ft at 3000rpm, max speed 107mph

0-60mph – 9.4 secs (*Car & Driver* Oct 1976)

Engine – water-cooled 2498cc/152cu in OHV six-in-line cylinders. Iron block & head. Bore – 74.7mm, stroke 95mm

Induction – twin side-draft Stromberg 175 1¾in carburettors

Transmission – 'J' type four-speed manual gearbox. Synchromesh fitted to all forward gears. Some cars were fitted with 'J' type overdrive units operating on top two gears

Ignition key fitted to and actuated a steering column lock.

Factory colours

Blues – Delft, French, Mallard, Royal, Sapphire, Tahiti

Browns – Maple, Russet, Sienna

Greens – British-Racing, Conifer, Emerald, Java, Laurel

Reds – Carmine, Damson, Magenta, Pimento, Signal

Whites – White

Yellows – Inca, Jasmine, Mimosa, Saffron, Topaz

The Essential Buyer's Guide™ series ...

978-1-845840-22-8

978-1-845840-26-6

978-1-845840-29-7

978-1-845840-77-8

978-1-845840-99-0

978-1-904788-70-6

978-1-845841-01-0

978-1-845841-19-5

978-1-845841-13-3

978-1-845841-35-5

978-1-845841-36-2

978-1-845841-38-6

978-1-845841-46-1

978-1-845841-47-8

978-1-845841-63-8

978-1-845841-65-2

978-1-845841-88-1

978-1-845841-92-8

978-1-845842-00-0

978-1-845842-04-8

978-1-845842-05-5

978-1-845842-70-3

978-1-845842-81-9

978-1-845842-83-3

978-1-845842-84-0

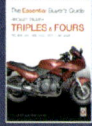
978-1-845842-87-1

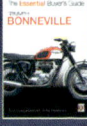
978-1-84584-134-8

978-1-845843-03-8

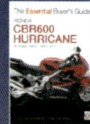
978-1-845843-09-0

978-1-845843-16-8

978-1-845843-29-8

978-1-845843-30-4

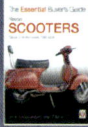
978-1-845843-34-2

978-1-845843-38-0

978-1-845843-39-7

978-1-845841-61-4

978-1-845842-31-4

978-1-845843-07-6

978-1-845843-40-3

978-1-845843-48-9

978-1-845843-63-2

978-1-845844-09-7

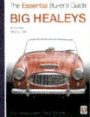

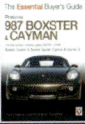

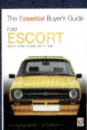

Also available from Veloce ...

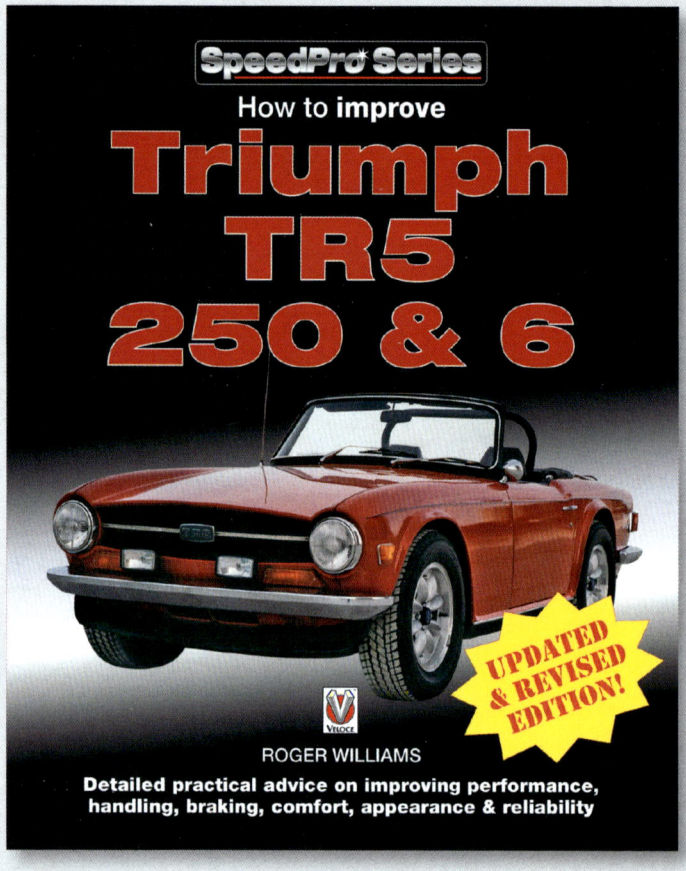

ISBN: 978-1-903706-46-6
Paperback • 27x20.7cm • £55* UK/$89.95* USA • 192 pages • 450+ colour
pictures

For more info on Veloce titles, visit our website at www.veloce.co.uk • email: info@
veloce.co.uk • Tel: +44(0)1305 260068
* prices subject to change, p&p extra

For more details on this or any Veloce title call 01305 260068, or visit
us on the web at www.veloce.co.uk

Index